Follow God, Not The Woman

Aaron Fields

TABLE OF CONTENTS

Something To Think About Before You Read

"There is only one influence that can bring good, prosperity, fulfillment, and peace in a man's life, and that is the influence of God & the holy spirit."

----------*Aaron Fields*

Word From The Author

In life, there are many obstacles that black men have to overcome. One of the major stumbling blocks that can prevent the black man from achieving high levels of success is going to be the woman. It's important for black men to understand that the vast majority of women are going to be nothing but a big distraction. Now, with that being said, is the woman a blessing? Yes, she is because God created her. However, it's important for the black man to understand that sometimes a blessing can also be a curse.

Can a woman also be a curse? Yes, she can, which is why black men must pay close attention to the type of women they bring into their lives. If you're a man seeking God, knowledge and wisdom, it's important that you don't place the woman on a pedestal. If you're a man of knowledge and wisdom that adheres to the scriptures, it's imperative that the woman follows you. Although women are beautiful human beings, they are not on the same level as God.

Unfortunately, in the black community, society has given all the power to the women. Therefore, not only is the black man acting and thinking like a woman, he's also placing the woman (black woman) as his God. When a black man thinks like a woman, he cannot lead and teach his woman. As a result, the black man will constantly find himself in these emotional arguments and meaningless fights that will never lead to anything constructive. That's why it's extremely important for you as a black man to not go back and forth in these silly arguments with women because all they're doing is distracting you.

The Fall Of Man (Genesis)

From a biblical perspective, the fall of man started once Adam put Eve over God. The reason Adam suffered wasn't because he didn't understand God. It was because he understood the laws of God, but he still put Eve on a pedestal. Understand that God will be the only consistent thing in your life, not the woman.

For those of you guys that are spiritual, you'll know that in the book of genesis (Adam & Eve), Satan came into the garden to trick and manipulate Eve, not Adam. Why? Well, from a biblical standpoint, in order to destroy the man, you have to contaminate and corrupt the woman.

As a man, you can't put the woman on a pedestal like Adam did in the bible. If you do, you'll try to appease and pacify women every time, which is not healthy. That's why Satan focused on tricking the woman, because Satan knew Adam revered Eve. If a man worships a woman, he'll do anything she wants.

This biblical concept also applies to the black man. Think about it, a major reason the black community is in disarray right now is because black women are being worshipped and too many men have been putting them on a pedestal just like Adam. From a societal perspective, in order to destroy the black man, you have to exalt the woman, feed her ego and give her different ideologies to embrace and conform to.

In the black community, the woman is ahead of God and the man, which is not correct. From a biblical standpoint, the chain of command is God, Christ, man, woman, child. Why? Well, it's because when the man is in his right state of mind, and he's spiritually mature, he's going to know how to keep things peaceful and in order. Your job as a man is to love, honor,

respect, and cherish your woman, not become overly infatuated with her. That's why God got

upset with Adam because he put Eve on a pedestal by putting her ahead of God.

How Does The Enemy Operate?

In life, most enemies operate by pursuing the ones that are easily susceptible to manipulation. In genesis, Eve was the one that easily fell into deception. If you think about it, this concept still applies in society today because most women are more likely to reason with most things, even if it's ungodly.

When you read (1 Timothy 2.14), it'll tell you that Adam wasn't deceived, but Eve was being deceived. In the bible, Adam clearly knew that he was not supposed to eat from that particular tree in the midst of the garden, but he did it anyway. Why did he do it? It's because he thought Eve was ahead of God.

Although it's important to honor, love, and cherish the woman, you still have to remain separate from her when it comes to fulfilling the mission for God. For the men reading this, i hope and pray that this speaks volume to you. Always remember that anytime when you're dealing with a woman on a serious level, you as the man are responsible for her. Why? Well, because from a biblical standpoint the onus will always be on you because the woman by nature is unpredictable, whimsical, and capricious. The onus is on you because God placed you as the leader and the head.

Follow God No Matter What

As a black man, when it comes to dealing with women and your decision makings, always stay alert and be mindful of the circumstances you're in. As a man, when the most high God speaks to you and shows you the truth on how he wants you to lead your community, your family, and your woman/wife, you must stick to it no matter what. When it comes to your woman, don't be afraid to lead her. If she has no interest in you being the leader and she doesn't respect you as a male authority figure, consider moving on and ending the relationship.

Being the head and the leader as a man does not make you an evil person. Don't conform to what society tells you because their agenda is to exalt and glorify the woman. When it comes to obeying the laws of God, don't heed the voice of the woman when she's going against the will of God.

When you look into **Genesis 3:17-19**, God turns to Adam and gives him a severe punishment which resulted in Adam having to do extremely hard physical labor in the land. Instead of Adam easily planting seeds and producing crops in the garden, the ground is now cursed. Therefore, Adam will suffer and struggle in getting the ground to produce edible foods.

When you compare Adam's punishment to Eve and the Serpent, you'll notice that Adam's curse was a lot longer and more detailed. Why is that? Well, it's because as a man, Adam failed to protect and lead his woman.

What Can We Learn From Adam?

If God's word backs up the direction in which God is entrusting you as the man to lead your woman, then it must be your obligation. When it comes to obeying God, it doesn't matter what society says, and it doesn't matter what the woman says. Why? Well, because as a black man, if you don't heed the word of God, you'll suffer the consequences like Adam did. Let's be honest as a black man, the vast majority of the women are going to blame you for everything anyway, so you might as well take the lead and carry out the mission.

As a man, you are the head, and the woman is the body or your help meet. Now I'm not saying you should never listen to your woman because if she's a wonderful human being, and she respects God's orders, it's okay to trust her. However, when you hear from the most high God and follow him, it may be difficult for most women to comprehend God's mission. As a result, the woman may bring chaos and confusion into your life, even if she doesn't realize it.

One of the major reasons why black men are at the bottom of the totem pole in this society is largely because many of them put women on a pedestal. Not only many of them fear women, but they worship them as well, which is not healthy and truthful. Keep in mind, Adam made the mistake of not correcting and speaking truth to his wife Eve when she misled him, because he was with her. Unfortunately, many black men can relate to this because many of them struggle with discipline and temptation. Anytime a woman wants you to partake in sinful behaviors with her, she's not a virtuous woman. If you're a black man that continues to seek knowledge and wisdom from God, the vast majority of women will look at you in a strange way, and that's okay, because society doesn't believe that black men can be astute, upstanding, and spiritual. When it comes to the woman, all you can do is keep her in prayer and hope that one day God will shape her heart. If the woman refuses to listen and she continues to disrespect you, all you have to do is leave the relationship and move on with your life.

Be Careful Around Certain Women

Have you noticed that in the black community, the woman dictates everything. That's because this demonic society has trademarked all the power to the woman. As a result, the black man thinks like a woman. Please understand that when a man acts and thinks like a woman, he won't be able to read the woman. When a man acts like a woman, he'll continue to find himself in many of these emotional, endless, and meaningless fights. Once again, that's why it's important for black men to not go back and forth with women.

Most of you guys are going to encounter women that are mentally unstable, emotionally fractured, and psychologically disturbed. I implore you guys to be aware of your surroundings and please pay close attention to the way you interact with certain women. Why am I saying this? It's because most of the toxic situations you guys find yourselves in with these women could have easily been avoided if you were thinking with your head and not your penis.

As black men, please understand that none of us are perfect. We've all been in tough situations before. We've all experienced at least one moment of weakness in our lives. However, it's important that we learn and grow from our mistakes. It's also important that we all continue to elevate ourselves to a higher level of existence because that's what life is about.

Have you ever been in a toxic relationship or in a dangerous situation with a woman that could have easily been avoided? If so, what was your experience like? What did you learn from your experience? Moving forward, how do you plan on elevating your level of existence?

_____

_____

_____

_____

_____

_____

_____

_____

_____

_____

_____

_____

_____

_____

_____

_____

You Can't Turn A Whore Into A Wife

Gentlemen, if you see a woman with many red flags, don't make her your girlfriend or wife. Keep in mind, you're always doing yourself a disservice when you ignore red flags. Why. Well, because in the end, those red flags will eventually come back to bite on the backside.

When you see major red flags in a woman, don't pretend that things are okay, and then suddenly try to change her. For the most part, what you see in these women is what you're going to get. As a man, you can never force a woman to change into something that she doesn't want to be. In order for the woman to change, she has to do it herself.

Please understand that the vast majority of these modern women that you guys are dealing with have no interest in wanting to change. Most women in this society do not want to convert from being a whore to a wife and a loving mother. Why? Well, because unlike the whore, the wife will get far less media attention, less publicity, and more responsibilities. Most modern women in this society not only seek attention, but they are also infatuated with advertising themselves sexually. Many of these women not only walk around with a sense of entitlement, but they want to be worshipped as well.

Even though it's important to treat women with love and respect, always pay attention to the women you bring into your life. As a man, what were some major red flags you've noticed when you were with a woman? Did you ignore these red flags or addressed them? How did these red flags affect your relationship with her? (in a positive or negative way)

_____

_____

_____

_____

_____

_____

_____

_____

_____

_____

_____

_____

_____

_____

_____

_____

_____

Don't Stay With A Toxic Woman

Anytime a man is choosing to deal with a toxic woman, the onus is on him. When it comes to toxic relationships, the responsibility always starts with the man, not the woman. Why is that? It's because as men, we have the power and the opportunity to create the lives that we want. Believe it or not, there are certain things that you as a man don't have to tolerate.

As a man, you don't have to stick around with a toxic woman just because she has a pretty face and a nice body. When you keep these toxic women around you, you're enabling them to bring more chaos and confusion into your life. Anytime you continue to fool around with a low-quality woman, chances are it'll lead to your demise.

If it's not meant to work out with a certain woman, move on. In life, you can't reclaim something if it's not meant to be reclaimed. When you try to make things work with a toxic woman, your life is going to be a living hell. As a man, if you're not careful, some of these women may end up hurting you or they may even attempt to file false allegations against you. The reason you guys get caught up in these situations is because many of you put women on a pedestal. Many of you guys are afraid to establish the rules of engagement. Although women are gorgeous and wonderful human beings, many of them are delusional and have a demonic spirit. That's why it's important for you guys to seek knowledge and wisdom from teachers and elders so you can know how to operate around women.

11

Why do you think most men choose to stay in these toxic relationships with women? Why do most men have the tendency to normalize destructive behavior from these women?

_____

_____

_____

_____

_____

_____

_____

_____

_____

_____

_____

_____

_____

_____

_____

_____

_____

_____

8

Don't Be Afraid To Be A Leader

I must admit, many of you guys are highly intelligent whether you realize it or not. Although it's a great thing that many of you guys are seeking worldly intelligence, I encourage you all to seek spiritual intelligence as well. In my honest opinion, lacking spiritual intelligence is one of the many reasons many black men are afraid to lead.

Even though black men are extremely smart, a large part of their intelligence is not coming from the inspiration of God. Unfortunately, most black men have a carnal mindset. What do I mean by that? It means that most black men would rather put more focus on the physical things and the sexual needs of women as opposed to adhering to the laws of God. As a result, you have black men putting women on a pedestal.

One of the major reasons most black men are at the bottom of the totem pole in this society is because they love to worship women. Not only do they love to worship women, they're also scared of women. Why do I say that? Think about it, when you worship something, that means you will show great fear of it.

Believe it or not, most women already know that many of you guys love worshiping them, that's why they don't respect you. Even though most women are always talking about wanting a "real man", they also enjoy receiving unnecessary attention from you guys because they know most men will idolize them. Therefore, most women not only worship themselves, but they try to reinforce society to worship them as well (**idolatry**), which makes them a narcissist.

I truly believe that all black men have great leadership capabilities. However, most black men don't have true confidence in themselves. Why is that? It's because most black men have been programmed and conditioned to be content with women leading them. As it pertains to the black community, most black men have been trained to obey and buy into the black matriarchy. The point that I'm trying to make is that many of you guys are highly intelligent and fully capable of leading the way. All you need to do is believe in yourself and step up to the plate.

Leave Your Comfort Zone

It's unfortunate that many black men are content with not being leaders in the community and in the household. Once again, a lot of you guys have so much potential to lead your people. Other than being obsessed with women, another reason many black men are not interested in leadership is because many of them are not disciplined.

No disrespect, but if I'm being honest, most black men struggle with discipline. Many of you guys are struggling with drugs, alcohol, food, and women. Now does this apply to all of you? No, it does not because there are exceptions to the rule.

Not only black men struggle with discipline, black men are also easily susceptible to conforming to different ideologies that are taking place in this society. This largely explains why the black community is so dysfunctional right now. Without the black man's leadership, his community starts embracing new ideas that are not biblical. As a result, these new ideas end up harming the black community.

With everything going on in this society, what is the black man going to do? How will he lead his people? When will he tell his woman to follow him? When will he believe in himself? When will he stop conforming to these different ideologies? When will he stop worshipping women? When will he leave his comfort zone and follow God?

Serving God

Serving God is not a top priority in most black men's lives. Most black men don't adhere to the scriptures because they spend most of their time on social media, using drugs, drinking too much alcohol, conforming to society, chasing booty and going back and forth with women. Yet, black men wonder why their faith is not strong.

In life, you can't give so little to something and then expect so much in return. In life, you can't walk around in self-defeat, feeling angry at the world because they won't accept you. In life, you cannot seek validation from a society that doesn't care about you. The only entity that the black man should seek is the most high God. Why? Well, because God is the only thing in this world that will not only create peace and fulfillment in his life. God will also bring truth, clarity and sanity within his spirit.

Keep in mind that it's impossible to revere God, believe in the scriptures, and obey his laws when you don't have faith. As a black man, if you choose to replace God with a woman, your life will go downhill. Yes, women are lovely and beautiful, but please understand that women are not adequate substitutes for God. If you are seeking any level of truth and understanding in this world, you need God in your life. In order to lead a purposeful and fulfilling life, God needs to be at the center stage of your life, not women.

What Are You Hungry For?

Although spending quality time with a beautiful woman is fun and desirable, having a hunger for God and for righteousness is way more valuable. Having a hunger for God gives you a certain level of knowledge and wisdom that a woman can never give you. As a man, when you develop an unhealthy yearning for women, you compromise yourself mentally, emotionally, and spiritually.

The longing to maintain a strong connection with the most high God is not only a blessing, but a gift. It is impossible for a man to know God in his fullness if he's overly infatuated with women. As a man, if you're allowing women to come into your life to take up all your time to where you don't have enough time to pray, meditate or fulfill God's purpose, you're making a big mistake. A man that is trying to elevate to a higher level of existence should never put the woman before God.

To arrive at a point where seeking knowledge and wisdom from God is not a priority is truly a spiritual tragedy. Many black men do not truly understand the nature of women. That's why most black men are walking around feeling self-defeated and perplexed. Once the black man finally wakes up and learns from his past traumatic experiences with women, he may start to feel ashamed of his own ignorance. Gentlemen, please understand that none of us are perfect because in our lives we will make mistakes. However, it's important that you learn and move on so you can focus on elevating your life. I promise you, once you understand the nature of the woman, you won't have time to show any anger, bitterness, or resentment towards her because you'll be more focused on finding peace and fulfillment in your own life.

Don't Get Distracted

Yes, women are beautiful, but if you're not careful, most women will use their outward beauty to distract you. Women will use things such as butt implants, boob jobs, hair extension, and makeup to distract you. As a man, you must know these things because the Lord knows that in most cases women will use their physical attributes to bring chaos, confusion, and corruption. Therefore, you allow the woman to steer you away from your purpose in life.

Now if you're the type of guy that's not easily distracted by women, don't assume you'll be off the hook. In fact, a man that's not easily distracted by women must maintain a watchful eye at all times. Why is that? Well, when most women know they can't overcome a man with their physical appearance, they'll have to be clever and crafty in multiple ways in order to manipulate him.

Once again, please be extremely careful around women and their outward appearances because many of them are wicked on the inside. Always stay alert and please understand that even if they don't trick you or fool you with their physical beauty, they will attempt to manipulate you in other ways. Just because the woman presents herself as this "godly woman" doesn't mean she is telling the truth. Remember, the nature of the woman is that she's whimsical, capricious, and manipulative. Once you start a serious relationship with a woman, don't be surprised when she shows you her true colors. Don't get upset when the woman presents herself as an ungodly woman, because the reality is that there are few virtuous women in this society.

Be Wary Of The "Spiritual Woman"

As a black man, a major phenomenon you have to be wary of is the "spiritual woman". As society continues to go downhill, you're going to have a lot of women come into your life and claim that they are "different" or "they're not like other women". Don't be surprised when you hear the vast majority of women say they "believe" in the bible.

Not only is the woman is whimsical, capricious and manipulative, the woman is also a survivor. What exactly do I mean by that? When I say a woman is a survivor by nature, it means that she is easily susceptible to getting manipulated and changing who she is in order to survive in her environment. Please understand that the woman is willing to adapt by any means necessary, which means that most of the things a woman says to you will be a lie.

As society crumbles, you're going to see more of these "spiritual women" looking for a man. Even if the woman you're dealing with really is spiritual, you as a man should still take your time with her. Why? Well, because it's important to get to know her and understand what she's really about. As a man, please be aware that at any moment, the woman can suddenly change up on you because that's her essential nature.

If you're a man and you're constantly seeking knowledge, wisdom, and guidance from the most high God, consider it to be a blessing. When women see you as a man of God, not only they'll view you as a rare figure, but they'll also become happy the more they're around you. If you're a man and this applies to you, please use your power and your gifts appropriately and accordingly. Once again, when you encounter a "spiritual woman" and she believes the man should be her head and she believes in the scriptures, please take your time with her anyway because many of these women are bluffing and they're desperate. When life gets tough for the

woman, she's going to reach out to certain men for subsistence, support, and stability

How To Conquer Your Adversaries

When a man's level of faith is strong and active, it becomes highly possible for him to conquer Satan and his evil forces. Sometimes Satan will use a woman to undermine a man's authority, faith, joy, and peace. As a man, you must learn how to reject toxic behavior. There is no shame in standing firm against all the wrong ideologies that women may try to put in your mind. In order to achieve this, use the knowledge and wisdom God has given you.

Believe it or not, you as a man have the spiritual authority to omit any negative thought and reject any individual or authority figure in your life that seeks to go against the will of God. Take the time to pray and ask the most high God for spiritual guidance. In order to stand firm against Satan's schemes, don't be afraid to put on the full armor of God.

When a man has faith and adheres to the scriptures, nothing in this world can oppress him. As a man, always use the spiritual tools God has given you in order to stand firm against the enemy. Through faith, you have the godly authority to overcome anything your adversary throws at you.

Protect Yourself At All Times

Gentlemen, it's important to understand that most of the women you guys choose to have relationships with are going to be carrying a lot of baggage from their previous relationships. Keep in mind that, in this current society that we're in, you're going to encounter many "liberated" women who have been intimate or sexual on many different occasions with both men and women before meeting you. No disrespect, but most of these women usually seek to be in a toxic relationship with a degenerate. If you're a pretty stabled individual with a bright future ahead of you, be careful with these types of women. Why? Well, because whatever issues the woman had in her previous relationships can easily affect your life negatively. If you're not careful, many of these women can ruin your life, that's why you should always put God ahead of the woman.

Yes, even though there are many women that love to bring chaos and destruction into a man's life, the onus is still on you as a man because you have the power and the authority to walk away from them. Just because she's a woman with a pretty face and a nice body, it doesn't mean you have to stay and tolerate her nonsense. With that being said, never allow your bitterness, anger, and hatred towards women take over, causing you to say or do regretful things. Grow in stature by loving women from afar and praying for them. If you need to cut ties with these women, please do so because you don't want any more dangerous situation with them that will ruin your life.

Most women that don't have insight into your spiritual nature may find your behavior rather strange and weird. However, you as a man will know that by being spiritually mature, you yourself will recognize the benefits of putting God above the woman. As a man, when you decide to follow God instead of the woman, you'll be guided into new heights of true satisfaction and self-fulfillment.

Once again, stay alert and be on the lookout when it comes to dealing with women. Please protect your mind, spirit, and your soul. As a black man, make sure you know who you are, your purpose in life, and the reason for your existence in this world. If you don't know who you are, you easily become susceptible to being manipulated by women. As long as you keep God in your heart first, you'll never have to worry about a woman taking over your life because most of them have a hidden agenda and will do anything they can to steer you off course.

What are some things that you learned from this book? What were some things that you didn't know prior to reading this book? Moving forward, how do you plan on elevating your level of existence?

ABOUT THE AUTHOR

Aaron Fields is the founder and owner of The Write Perspective, LLC. He gives great advice to children and adults on how to enlarge their freedom and opportunities by helping them change and improve certain aspects of their personal, professional, and spiritual lives. Aaron Fields graduated from the University of Texas at Dallas with a bachelor of science in Speech Language Pathology & Child Development and a master's degree in Human Development and Early Childhood Disorder.

The purpose of The Write Perspective is to serve the personal, social, & or spiritual development needs of individuals who have the desire to learn, grow, and develop the right perspective. Aaron Fields resides in the state of Texas where he continues to write his books and blogs with the explicit intention of helping his readers and audience to change or improve some aspects of their personal, professional and spiritual lives. Aaron Fields travels to 50+ cities a year in the United States and abroad to help others understand their identity, create their purpose and how to utilize their gifts and talents for the betterment of humanity. During his travels, Aaron Fields inspires and mobilizes in early childhood centers, schools, colleges, juvenile facilities, prison, churches, and community neighborhoods. In addition to his books and public events, Aaron Fields spends a great portion of his time improving the health and well-being of young children as an Early Childhood Consultant because he believes in unlocking the true potential of the youth.

STAYING CONNECTED

Share Your Story

Email me at **authoraaronfields@gmail.com** and share your thoughts about this book. Feel free to also share your story and personal breakthrough. Let me know how ***Follow God, Not The Woman*** has affected your life.

Allow Me to Partner With You

Need a mentor/life coach? I'm ready to walk with you through the process. Email me at **authoraaronfields@gmail.com** or visit twperspective.com, select life/spiritual coach and book your session today!

Need a Speaker?

Are you looking for a dynamic speaker for an upcoming conference, organizational training event, or workshop? Visit twperspective.com

Follow Me

twperspective.com – visit me here to order additional copies of ***Follow God, Not The Woman*** and gain insight into all of the resources The Write Perspective offers individuals and organizations.

Instagram: _twperspective

Twitter: @_TWPerspective

Linked In: https//www.linkedin.com/in/aaron-fields-022092104

Notes

A man should never pin his whole faith on a woman.

Yes, there are many wonderful things you can do with a woman.

However, you should never build your self-worth around her.

Why? Because your self-worth comes from God

----------Aaron Fields

Printed in Great Britain
by Amazon

86127807R00020